Million Dollar Butterflies

Children in Business

———————

Mary L. MacNeilly

If nothing ever
changed,
there'd be no
butterflies...

What is a million dollar butterfly?

A million dollar butterfly is a kid who runs their own business.

Starting a business is hard, but fun
Read this book and learn how it's done

Hear from five kids who are just like you
Who built a business & made their dreams come true

They wrote their own stories and shared them with me
Then I put them in here for you to see!

For music videos, songs, and more stories like these,
Go online now and connect with us please!

 Miss Mary

www.milliondollarbutterflies.com

A story from Evan:

A few days ago I was at a marketing event with my mom. Next to her friend was a booth for American Family Insurance. I went over to them and sang the jingle. They liked that, and asked me if I would walk around and sing it. I said, "Sure." I did that, and came back. Then we made a deal that I would pass out business cards to people there and they would pay me $5. I did it, and got paid. Then I had an idea to go around to some other people and see if they would pay me too. I did it a few more times and had $11.

I gave the money to my mom and asked her if I could do a few more. At first, she said no. Then she saw I was pretty disappointed about that, so she let me. I told her I wanted to make $16. She said ok. By the end of the night I had made $21, and I was pretty proud of myself. I had never made so much money in such a short time. There is another event next month and I am going to go to that one too and charge everyone $5. My goal is to make at least $30.

I had a great experience that night that taught me about making money and I think I'm going to start a new chapter in my life.

I guess it pays to have really good manners!

4

A story from Rylie:

Hello! My name is Rylie and my business is Dance to the Pointe. I always dreamed of writing a book that would be a survival guide for young dancers like me. I had several questions over the years like what kind of diet should a dancer follow? How can I juggle dance and school? Are there any exercises that would help me become a stronger dancer? When I went to the library to research these questions, I couldn't find a fun book with these answers!

About six months ago I created an outline for a book; I started filling in the outline, and chapters began to form. Then an amazing mentor came into my life and taught me I could write a book to help dancers **AND** actually start my own business! I completed a 2 day class on Extreme Business Building to start my business.

My mission is to offer dancers answers to their questions like how to stand out in an audition, how to perform on stage, what to eat, and fun need to know facts about dance. I will accomplish this by writing a fun book. I also have a clothing line! In the future I will offer workshops that offer lots of information and provide a fun place to dance.

My business will be successful because it offers a resource for younger dancers. Several teachers help them learn the right technique and how to learn a dance combination but rarely do they tell you the tricks to becoming a successful, well rounded dancer. You have to figure it out by yourself with trial and error.

My planning was fast and furious; mostly done in my Extreme Business Building class. I have budgeted to spend $500 to start my business and earn $5,000 in the first year. The market need caters to younger dancers. A similar magazine that caters to adult dancers has 20,000 likes on their Facebook page. That tells me there are thousands of dancers looking to read about their passion!

My operational structure begins with just me. I'll start by selling dancewear, and then publish my first book. I'll market my business by word of mouth, my website, Facebook page, and eventually a blog and YouTube channel to reach even more dancers.

Thank you for letting me **share** my new **business** with you! Please **check out** my **Facebook** page, **Dance to the Pointe**, and be on the **lookout** for my official clothing line **launch**!

A story from Miles:

Hi, my name is Miles and my company is Sushimee. I have been in business since 2007, I started it when I was 7. My mission is to build my business so it is on the S&P 500 someday. I like owning my own business and hope to save enough money to pay for my college education. I make candy sushi. It's a product made out of rice crispy treats and candy so it looks like the real thing. I sell it in a 5 piece bento box and I have 4 flavors of candy sushi.

So far my business is successful because the product is unique, but also because of perseverance. It's easy to want to give up when it gets hard, but I made it through some hard stuff and I have been successful because of that. Below is an outline of my initial planning process and strategy.

Financial Requirements & Goals: To start, I borrowed $20 from my Mom to buy the initial supply. I also used money from winning competitions to fund my business. Now I am doing a crowd sourcing campaign so I can grow the business even more.

Market Need & Opportunity: The candy industry is a growing industry. Last year it grew over $338 million dollars. Candy is always popular with kids, so I think that my product is a good one to market to kids and adults too.

Operational Structure: I am the founder and president of the company. My Mom helps me with contracts, other complicated things, and driving me to my deliveries. I do the candy production, deliveries, and sales for the business. When I have a big order, I hire a production person to fill the order or help me in the kitchen. In the past, I used to hire my friends, but now since the orders have gotten bigger, I hire kitchen professionals to help me.

Sales/Market Strategy: I pitch my product to locally owned candy stores and small places, like Ace Hardware, Coffee shops, Tony's Market, and Marczyk's Market. I also sell online and in December will start to do online ads like Google Ads. I also do one event per month, like in December; I am doing the Chocolate Festival in Colorado Springs at the Broadmoor Hotel.

A story from Lyla:

Hi, my name is Lyla and my business is Flour Gal. I had a dream: to bake special cupcakes for special people. That's why I created Flour Gal in 2010, when I was 10 years old. Armed with delectable recipes and a dedication to making cupcakes from scratch with the freshest ingredients, I am pursuing my mission to create smiles by the dozen.

I make the most delicious and artistic cupcakes you have ever seen. I make classic cupcakes like red velvet with cream cheese frosting, but I also make amazing specialty cupcakes like the Key Lime: vanilla cake filled with homemade key lime curd topped with fresh whipped cream frosting! I can also host birthday parties with cupcake decorating activities.

My business is successful because everyone loves cupcakes! I think it is in our DNA! People constantly need cupcakes for events including family gatherings, birthday parties to larger corporate functions. Below is an outline of my initial planning and strategy!

Financial Requirements: Through crowd-funding on FirstFunder.com, I raised $2000. I'll use this money to purchase bakery equipment, supplies, and to rent space in a commercial kitchen to increase volume.

Market Need & Opportunity: My market is people of all ages, gender, and interests who want a gourmet, moist, and unique cupcake. There are no individual cupcakes stores in my area. Also, people like to support young entrepreneurs in the community.

Operational Structure: The Flour Gal team includes me (CEO) and as we grow, my M-O-M is helping in the role of C-O-O. Our exit strategy consists of continuing to grow the company and eventually have it help pay for my college, and then begin franchising!

Sales/Market Strategy: I have community support through Young Americans Bank and Metropolitan State College of Denver. I've won awards for my business including 2012 Colorado Young Entrepreneurs Winner and 2012 Rockies Venture Club Colorado Capital Conference Youth Entrepreneurship Award. I've been featured on 9 News, Denver Post, and more. I am currently mentored by Kent Thiry, CEO of DaVita, a Fortune 500 kidney company.

7

A story from Tanner & Taylor:

Hi, our names are Tanner & Taylor, we own Alkaline Clothing. Our mission is to provide our customers with a high quality product while valuing each and every opinion to ensure satisfaction. Alkaline Clothing offers quality ring spun cotton t-shirts catered to young adults. Alkaline also offers custom imprints for businesses, schools, team etc. We believed that Alkaline would succeed because nobody in our town offered high quality custom printed products. We felt we could change that by taking the initiative to make a big effort in learning the process of screen printing and learning different techniques in order to make something different than the impersonal online shops. We also felt we could sell our own clothing line because we were living within the culture that we wanted to cater to and could see firsthand what was popular and what we believed would sell. Our strategy is outlined below.

Financial Requirements & Goals: We started Alkaline with $200 and bought our first batch of shirts and some screen printing supplies. We spent a lot of time learning the screen printing process through online tutorials in the beginning because it was cost effective and we learned the basics to provide a shirt that at least wouldn't wash out. Our initial screen printing supply investment was minimal (about $70) for the basics, we have since invested much more (roughly $3500) from sales. The first batch of shirts was a necessity and we began with a small batch (about 60 shirts for $130) where we printed our first logo and sold out very quickly. We took the money from the initial sales to purchase more shirts, marketing materials and eventually equipment. Our financial goals for the future are to continue investing money from sales into new equipment and education. Our near future goals are to get two major pieces of equipment, one being a new screen printing press (roughly $4500.) and a conveyor dryer (roughly $2500) along with software and other various supplies (roughly $1000). We plan to purchase these investments through the buildup of sales. All of the equipment we plan to purchase isn't a necessity for screen printing, however, it will make us much more efficient and will allow us to move at a faster pace and produce more intricate shirts which will allow us to offer more to our customers.

Market Need & Opportunity: The tees that were offered through clubs not only didn't contain a variety of different products or designs, but the ink itself would wash off the shirt. We were determined to provide not just our school but surrounding places with a high quality that wouldn't wash out. Along with providing custom shirts, we wanted to provide people our age with hand printed, local clothing catered to our age group.

Operational Structure: We knew Alkaline couldn't run the way we started forever. The way we were printing shirts could still produce a good quality, but we were determined to become more efficient and to keep improving our quality. So we took the necessary measures and planned out strategically the order we needed to upgrade our equipment. Then we financially planned what was necessary at the time, knowing we would upgrade everything at some point. We also went from printing wherever there was a free space to creating a functioning workshop. We created systems to get the job done. By being able to perfect the screen printing process we were able to create the most efficient systems. We operate in a specific order to ensure a faster production rate to grow our business faster. By creating systems we have not only allowed ourselves to move at a faster pace, but when the big orders come in and we bring in help, they are able to move at a faster pace and are able to understand the procedure that we operate in.

Sales/Market Strategy: Even though we produce a high quality product, we knew they wouldn't sell themselves. One thing we have focused on is our product packaging which is advertised through social media and our website. The superior packaging draws the buyer in and we have received great feedback. We package all of our t-shirts in a fitting linen bag imprinted with our logo. The bags are reusable so people see our logo more than just on the shirts. We chose to use linen bags rather than plastic bags because it is environmentally friendly, which is highly valued and the cost to produce the bags is just slightly higher than plastic bags. We also include stickers for people to put wherever they please which allows for more exposure. We give out free stickers to show our appreciation for the interest in our company whenever we attend events, personal functions or speeches. We also advertised in a Colorado action sports magazine catered to people in their mid-twenties, which is our general audience. We feel publicity leads to more sales than through direct marketing so we tend to focus more on articles, videos and social media.

Want to start your own business?

We would L♥VE for you to think about starting your own business! Just follow these steps!

List 3 things you're really good at doing:

1. _____
2. _____
3. _____

THEN PICK YOUR FAVORITE ONE!

How much do you charge?

YOUR TOTAL COST OF PRODUCT PER ITEM OR JOB: $_____

+ HOW MUCH $$ YOU WANT TO MAKE PER ITEM OR JOB: + $_____

= HOW MUCH MONEY YOU NEED TO SELL IT FOR!   = $_____

Who else is doing this? List 3 competitors & how much they charge!

1. _____ : $_____
2. _____ : $_____
3. _____ : $_____

How are you different? Do you cost more or less? Is your product or service better? How? Are you more fun to work with? List 3 ways you're different:

1. _____

2. _____

3. _____

How are you going to tell people about your product or service?

____ FACEBOOK   ____ YOU TUBE   ____ OTHER

____ TWITTER   ____ FLYERS   ____ OTHER

____ NETWORKING   ____ RADIO   ____ OTHER

____ TV   ____ EMAIL   ____ OTHER

____ PHONE CALLS   ____ COMMUNITY EVENT

How do you make money?

We call money you earn **"revenue"**, money you spend **"expenses"**, and money leftover **"profit"**.

Use this chart as a **"budget"** so you know how to **"forecast"** your money!

	Month 1	Month 2	Month 3	Month 4	Month 5	Month 6
Revenue Type 1						
Revenue Type 2						
TOTAL REVENUE						
Expense Type 1						
Expense Type 2						
Expense Type 3						
TOTAL EXPENSES						
PROFIT!						

How much money do you need to start? Where are you going to get the money?

_____

_____

_____

What are the first 5 things you need to do to get started?
Write your plan!

1) _____
_____
_____
_____

2) _____
_____
_____
_____

3) _____
_____
_____
_____

4) _____
_____
_____
_____

5) _____
_____
_____
_____

It's really important that you make enough time to run a business! Use the calendar below to "block out" time for your business!

Remember to block out time for school, sports/recreation activities, family/friend time, and sleeping!

	Monday	Tuesday	Wednesday	Thursday	Friday	Saturday	Sunday
7 am							
8 am							
9 am							
10 am							
11 am							
12 pm							
1 pm							
2 pm							
3 pm							
4 pm							
5 pm							
6 pm							
7 pm							
8 pm							

Million Dollar Butterflies Sing-a-Long!

Song: Children in Business

Music Video: http://youtube.com/c/milliondollarbutterflies

Featuring: Meg, Simon, and Lane!

Children in business, now we're butterflies. Children in business, the future's in our hands.
The caterpillars; they talk the talk, but the butterflies; they walk the walk.
Just cuz we're kids doesn't mean we don't know how to start a business and watch it grow!
Good grades at school was the just the start.
We asked our parents to play their part.
We talk money, business, and market demand.
Started on the corner with a lemonade stand!
We chose product, price, place and promotion.
Our marketing campaign caused a lot of commotion.
Run a business well and hard work will pay.
We're kids, we did it, and here's what we say:
Children in business, Now we're butterflies.
Children in business: This is how we fly!
Children in business, now we're butterflies.
Children in business, the future's in our hands!
Hey man, count me in, here we go!
My name's Lane, I dance on any surface.
Not just for fun; I dance with purpose.
My business is for kids, I donate what I make
after calculating the expenses it takes.
My name is Simon, your system technician.
My business is tech, I'm the techy magician
Yeah, we're kids, but we figured it out, now we stand here,
stand here and shout!
Future leaders are what we are. Innovators & child stars!
We'll work together & teach you how.
Build a business & run it now!
Million Dollar Butterflies. We're Million Dollar Butterflies.
Million Dollar Butterflies. Million Dollar Butterflies!

Meet the MDB Cast!

Our cast is filled with 43 actors, singers, and dancers!
Watch them on our interactive website and TV show!

Gordy   Gator   Violet   Allison

Lane   Tahli   Meg   Arielle

Hannah   Maddie   Annabelle   Makenna

Chelsee	Gus	Boston	Beauty
Rylie	Bianca	Sydney	Charles
Anna	Sierra	Gil	Ashliana
Alyssa	Makiah	Zack	Brandon

Calvin

Rylann

Kylie

Kennedy

Taylor

Sophia

Kira

Talia

Seth

Kathleen

Leah

Morghan

Anna

Josh

Simon

For full bios and fun facts, connect with us at
www.facebook.com/milliondollarbutterflies

Want to become a million dollar butterfly?

Learn more at www.milliondollarbutterflies.com!

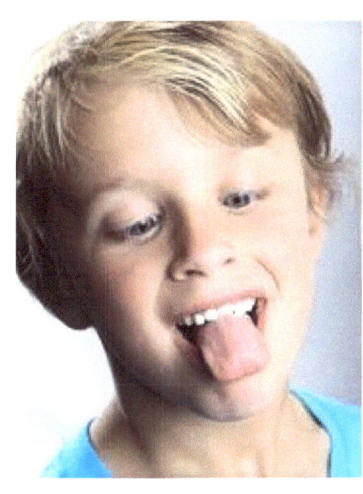

Hey Kids!

Get out your tongue and tell us your Young Entrepreneur story!

Be a part of the children's books Million Dollar Butterflies!

NOTES

NOTES

NOTES

NOTES

NOTES